3221

BABOONS

MONKEY DISCOVERY LIBRARY

Lynn M. Stone

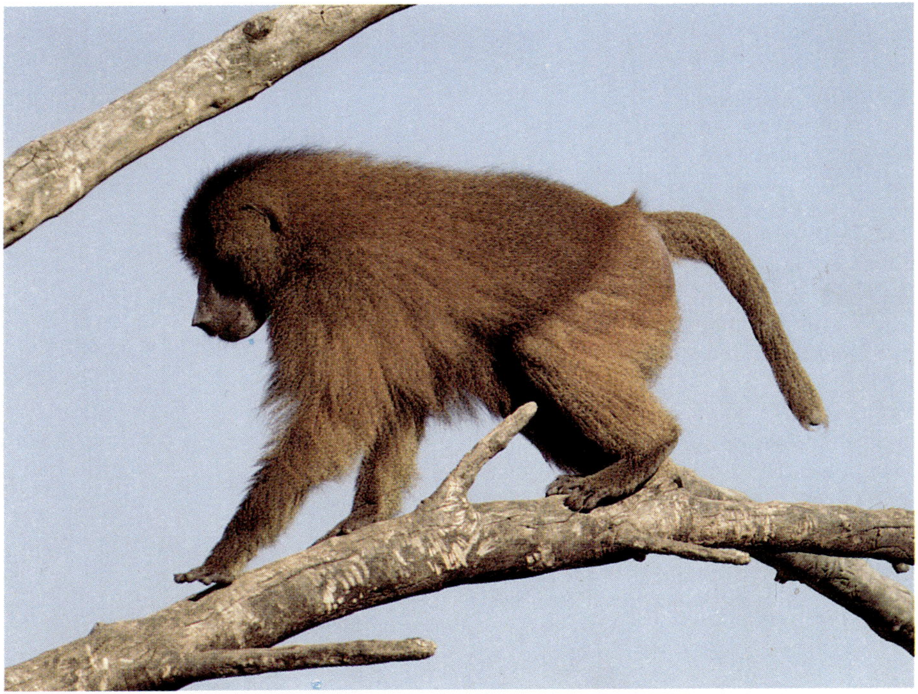

Rourke Corporation, Inc.
Vero Beach, Florida 32964

© 1990 Rourke Corporation, Inc.

All rights reserved. No part of this book may be reproduced or utilized in any form or by any means, electronic or mechanical including photocopying, recording or by any information storage and retrieval system without permission in writing from the publisher.

PHOTO CREDITS

All photos © Lynn M. Stone

ACKNOWLEDGEMENTS

The author thanks the following for photographic assistance: The Brookfield Zoo, Brookfield, Ill., Lowry Park Zoological Garden, Tampa, Fla.

LIBRARY OF CONGRESS
Library of Congress Cataloging-in-Publication Data
Stone, Lynn M.
   Baboons / by Lynn M. Stone.
     p. cm. — (Monkey discovery library)
   Summary: Describes the habitat, lifestyle, infancy, predators, relationship with humans, and future of this large African monkey.
   ISBN 0-86593-067-8
   1. Baboon—Juvenile literature. [1. Baboon.] I. Title. II. Series: Stone, Lynn M. Monkey discovery library.
QL737.P96S776   1990
599.88'44—dc20   90-31939
                                 CIP
                                  AC

TABLE OF CONTENTS

The Baboon	5
The Baboon's Cousins	6
How They Look	9
Where They Live	11
How They Live	14
The Baboon's Babies	16
Predator and Prey	19
The Baboon and People	20
The Baboon's Future	22
Glossary	23
Index	24

THE BABOON

No one likes to be called a baboon. "Baboon" makes us think of foolish behavior and being ugly.

Baboons are not very handsome to us. But people who study these large African monkeys know that they are not foolish.

Indeed, baboons are intelligent animals, and they show real concern toward each other.

Baboons live in groups called **troops.** Usually 30 to 60 baboons make up the troop.

Members of the troop have strong family ties. Baboons often help each other. They show real **affection** toward other baboons, too.

Guinea Baboon Troop

THE BABOON'S COUSINS

All eight **species,** or kinds, of baboons are related to monkeys and apes—gorillas, chimpanzees, and orangutans.

Monkeys and apes are among the animals which scientists call **primates.** Humans are also primates.

The larger primates have fingers and toes much like ours. They also have eyes which face forward and large brains. Some of them are the most intelligent animals on earth.

Orangutan

HOW THEY LOOK

A baboon looks like a heavyweight monkey with the **muzzle** of a dog. A baboon's muzzle, its mouth and jaws, sticks out.

Most baboons are brown or gray with white trim. But the adult male mandrill baboon is colorful. Its face looks like it was splashed by purple, blue, and red paint.

Male baboons often have long fur around their faces, like lions. Mandrill males wear a crest, too.

Baboons weigh from 30 to 120 pounds. Mandrills are the largest.

Male Mandrill Baboon

WHERE THEY LIVE

Baboons live only in Africa. One kind or another lives in almost every kind of place, or **habitat.**

Most species, such as the olive and guinea baboons, live in open places. They like woods with plenty of sunlight, grassland, and rocky hills.

The mandrill and the smaller drill baboons, however, live in dark, wet rain forests. The bright red rump of the male mandrill may work like a beacon in the dark forest. It may help other mandrills keep their leader in view.

Baboon in African Grassland

Male Guinea Baboon

Guinea Baboon Sleeping

HOW THEY LIVE

Baboons can climb well, but they spend most of their time on the ground.

They look for food, play, and **groom** their fur. People groom their hair with combs and brushes after a shampoo. Baboons groom each other with their fingers.

Grooming removes dirt, old skin, and insects. It also helps baboons make and keep friendships.

Members of a baboon troop usually stay together for a long time. Only the male leaders seem to change troops.

THE BABOON'S BABIES

A mother baboon usually has one baby. For six to eight months, it drinks its mother's milk.

The youngest baboons ride under their mother when they travel. Older babies cling to mom's back.

Growing up takes several years. Females are five years old before they have their first baby. Males don't become fathers before age seven.

A captive hamadryas baboon lived to be 37. A chacma baboon reached 45 years.

Guinea Baboon Troop

PREDATOR AND PREY

Most baboons eat plant and animal foods. Generally they eat whatever is most plentiful, such as grass, fruit, or nuts.

Baboons often travel two to five miles a day in search of food.

Baboons become **predators,** or hunters, when they attack other animals. The animals which baboons kill for food—rabbits, grasshoppers, baby antelope, and other small creatures—are their **prey.**

Baboons themselves are rarely prey for other predators. Baboons stay together and they can be quite fierce.

Baboon Eating

THE BABOON AND PEOPLE

Baboons are loud and quick to protect each other. People often feel unsafe near baboons.

Long ago, the people of Egypt made the hamadryas baboon part of their religion. But the hamadryas baboon is now **extinct**—completely gone—in Egypt. Modern Egyptians did not think highly of their baboons.

Most African people have never been fond of baboons. Many Africans fear and even hate baboons.

Guinea Baboon

THE BABOON'S FUTURE

Africa's wild places are shrinking as the human population grows. Many of Africa's wild animal populations are shrinking, too. It is not surprising that some of the baboon species are among them.

The gelada baboon has been hunted widely for its mane, which is used for headdresses and capes.

The drill and mandrill have been losing their forest home to wood cutters.

Like many of Africa's animals, baboons may some day survive only in national parks and zoos.

Glossary

affection (uh FEK shun)—a feeling of love and caring

extinct (ex TINKT)—the point at which an animal no longer exists

groom (GROOM)—to comb and clean fur by using the fingers

habitat (HAB a tat)—the kind of place in which an animal lives, such as grassland

muzzle (MUH zull)—the mouth, nose and jaws together

predator (PRED a tor)—an animal that kills other animals for food

prey (PRAY)—an animal that is hunted by another for food

primate (PRI mate)—the group of mammals which includes monkeys, apes, and man

species (SPEE sheez)—within a group of closely related animals, one certain kind

troop (TROOP)—a group of monkeys or apes

INDEX

age 16
babies 16
baboon, chacma 16
        drill 11, 22
        gelada 22
        guinea 11
        hamadryas 16, 20
        mandrill 9, 11, 22
        olive 11
color 9
face 9

food 19
fur 9, 14
grooming 14
habitat 11, 22
intelligence 5
monkey 5, 6, 9
prey 19
primates 6
species 6
troop 5, 14
weight 9

DATE DUE			
MAY 0 8 1991 101			
101 MAY 1 4 1991			
230 OCT 7 108			
JAN 21 1992			
JAN 28 1992 102			
MAR 28 1993 102			
APR 22 1993 106			
MR 15 '95 108			
MR 11 '96 109			
205 DE 14 '98			
JA U 5 '99 109			
OC 12 '00			
NO 15 '02			

HIGHSMITH 45-220